MESSAGES TO A NATION IN CRISIS

An Introduction to the Prophecy of Jeremiah

Steven M. Fettke

UNIVERSITY
PRESS OF
AMERICA

University Press of America, Inc."

P.O. Box 19101, Washington, D.C. 20036

Printed in the United States of America

ISBN (Perfect): 0-8191-2839-2

Library of Congress Number 82-19997

To my father, Merle Fettke, whose love
of God and His Word served as a shining example
to his family and friends.

iii

iv

Special thanks go to my mother, Lorraine V.B. Fettke, who sacrificially put me through seminary, my wife, Lorraine K. Fettke, who encourages me daily, and my friends and students who give me confidence and friendship.

Special thanks also go to Lynn Campbell for her excellent typing and Rusty DeBord for .the maps.

Contents

Preface

Introduction

The Messages

Preface

The purpose of this author was not to present an exhaustive verse-by-verse commentary on the book of Jeremiah. This book is meant to serve as an introduction to Jeremiah the man, and to introduce some of the major themes of his preaching. In the sermons of Jeremiah one can readily find guiding principles by which all people can order their lives. The sermons of this one man have made lasting impressions on men and women for centuries. In the light of this one cannot help but attempt to grasp at least the essence of what Jeremiah was speaking to the people of his day.

Although this book is meant to guide the beginning student of Jeremiah's sermons into a better understanding of what he meant to convey, it is no easy task to sort out all that he was speaking. But if one listens closely he will hear a faint cry from the distant past challenging his thought and faith:

> To whom shall I speak and give warning
> that they may hear? (6:10a)

Steven M. Fettke

I. Jeremiah, the Man

In the course of the events of history those nations which have endured national crises have done so in many cases by the great courage and strength of heroic leaders who were willing to defy popular opinion and often overwhelming odds. Jeremiah was such an individual; however, he won no victories, had no large following, nor received any accolades for his achievements during his lifetime. His calling was not to the field of battle nor to the arena of politics. He was called to restore the moral and spiritual integrity of the chosen people of Yahweh.* Despite persecution and stiff opposition from every level of society he urgently and patiently championed his cause for truth and justice for over forty years. The memory of few great leaders has been worthy of record or study. But Jeremiah's life and message still speaks volumes to all ·humankind.

We find in chapter one, verse one that Jeremiah was the son of Hilkiah, the priest. Although Hilkiah was not an uncommon name during the time, it is not unreasonable to assume Jeremiah was the son of the high priest Hilkiah, who had discovered the book of the

---

* The word used for God is His personal name, Yahweh, used in many places in the Old Testament, probably to be vocalized "Yahweh" (Yáhway). This is the word used by God in Exodus 3:14 to describe Himself to Moses. Many Jews still regard this name for God so holy that the word "Adonai" (Lord) is used in its place when reading the scriptures. This writer hopes that the use of God's own personal designation will help the reader reflect on the history of God's dealings with His people, and that he will realize the close relationship Jeremiah seems to have had with this great "I Am", Yahweh.

1

Law in the wall of the Temple during the reform of King Josiah (II Kings 22:8-13).[1] We
can see evidence of this possibility in the
respect accorded Jeremiah by the successive
kings of Judah and the officials of the government. His name also reflects the deeply religious heritage of his family. It probably
means "Yahweh has thrown", referring to the
beginning of Moses' song of triumph of Exodus
15, although there are other possibilities
for its meaning.[2]

Jeremiah's home town of Anathoth was one
of the ancient cities assigned to priests by
Joshua (Joshua 21:18), as commanded by Moses
(Numbers 35:2). This village was only about
three or four miles northeast of Jerusalem.
Although little is mentioned of Jeremiah's
early years, much can be inferred by what has
been revealed. He lived very near Jerusalem,
a religious, cultural, and trade center for
most of Palestine during his life. It was
easy for a young man to sense the political
and religious climate of the day by his constant contact with the events occuring in
Jerusalem, and the news from around the
known world brought by caravans of traders.

Jeremiah was probably most profoundly
influenced by the piety of his family. This
can be seen by the reference to Yahweh in
his name, as well as the obvious influence
of his father the priest. From his sermons
one can see that he was obviously well educated for a man of his day, especially in
the Law and Prophets. The reader can easily
detect his affinity for and spiritual kinship
with the eighth century prophet Hosea in his
deep concern over the unfaithfulness of Israel toward God (3:1). From the Law he is
most concerned with Israel's lack of adher-
ence to the regulations of Deuteronomy, and
God's punishment for this infidelity (7:4-11).

The call of Jeremiah was somewhat unique

2

among the prophets of Israel in that there was no burning bush (Moses), nor miraculous birth (Samuel), nor spectacular vision (Isaiah). Jeremiah's call is recorded as a simple dialogue between Yahweh and a young man. There is not even any indication that this was an audible conversation, but simply a deep inner knowledge of what Yahweh wanted him to do.

The time of this experience was 627 B.C., as indicated in 1:2. This was in the early years of Josiah's reform, which became the very object of Jeremiah's task, to try to restore his people to the ancient principles set forth by Moses in the Law.

Although this call experience was not particularly spectacular, it was, neverthe-less, quite overwhelming to this young man. He was not quite prepared to accept the re-sponsibility of such a far-reaching task. Preaching the reforms of Yahweh "to the na-tions" (1:5) was a bit more than he could ·grasp. With this in mind his reluctance in accepting this call is understandable. Yet he is comforted by a sense of Yahweh's help and presence to complete his task.

It is interesting that this call exper-ience serves as an introduction to the book. In it Yahweh gives Jeremiah the direction of his ministry; he was to go and speak as Yahweh commanded him (1:7). He is also given the em-phasis or purpose of his ministry; he was to both overthrow and plant kingdoms by his preach-ing (1:10). Finally, Yahweh gives him courage and authority by "touching" his mouth in that he is given the ability to speak (1:6,9). This was an anthropomorphic way of expressing Yah-weh's approval of Jeremiah's preaching and is reminiscent of earlier prophets (Deut. 18:18; Isaiah 6:6,7; Ezekiel 2:9-3:3).

It is this preaching of Jeremiah that bears

3

special attention. His tremendous ability to
speak in the name of Yahweh brought him the
attention of the entire nation for many years.
Yet most were so set in their pagan ways that
few responded positively to his preaching.
Most of the time Jeremiah met stiff opposition
to his preaching from the successive leadership
during his lifetime. Despite this opposition
Jeremiah stubbornly refused to alter his message or to cease from speaking. He was ridi-
culed, humiliated before the royal court, imprisoned (once in a muddy cistern), almost
killed by men of his own village, and put in
stocks for public display. Still his message
of reform from polytheism to the monotheism
of the ancients rang loud and clear.

But Jeremiah was not a man without dis-
couragement. He was a man of deep feeling who
always spoke with the passion and fervor of
a man totally immersed in his message, completely devoted to Yahweh and his people. He
often wept (9:1,18: 14:17) over the plight of
his countrymen, and, as a result, is often
called the weeping prophet. In fact, the
Lamentations of Jeremiah are a record of the
anguish he felt for a people who had gone into
the Babylonian captivity as punishment for
their unfaithfulness to Yahweh, despite his
many years of warning.

He also is known for his impassioned pleas
to Yahweh on behalf of Judah. He cries out
to Yahweh for His mercy and help, despite
the obvious rebellion and faithlessness of
the people. He takes the place of his people
before Yahweh and speaks as though he were
one with them (14:19-22).

Although a shining example of faith and
compassion, Jeremiah is not without fault.
As he struggled through the persecution and
humiliation of his faith and message, he sometimes would lash out against the One who had
called him. After being beaten and put in

4

the public stocks for his message, Jeremiah is overcome by despair and accused Yahweh of deceiving him (20:7-10). He sinks further into his depression by identifying with Job (Job 3:3-6) in that he curses the day of his birth and laments over the shame he has experienced (20:14-18).

As he often struggled through these crises of faith, it is to Jeremiah's credit that he did not long remain in despair. More often than not, this brave orator would find reason to praise the One whom he served. If he could accuse Yahweh, he could also sing praises to him (20:13). In the worst possible circumstances he could still worship Him and look for a better day (30:10, 11, 18-22).

The content of a man's message is a good part the man himself, and not just his words. In the school of Yahweh's prophets throughout the centuries Jeremiah is one of the headmasters. He brings honor to the prophetic institution simply by his strength of char-·acter and unwavering devotion.

His sterling character and dedication to his task can be seen in various incidents in the book. In one incident Jeremiah learns of a plot against his life. That fact was bad enough, but what was more tragic was that the men involved were from his home town, Anathoth (11:18-23). His own friends had demanded he stop prophesying (11:21). Yahweh's messages were scorned by the people, and the one who would try to convict them of wrong would suffer! Jeremiah is terribly hurt, yet realizes Yahweh will vindicate him (11:22,23).

In another incident Jeremiah is severely beaten and put into the public stocks for his preaching (20:1,2). This treatment was reserved for the common criminal so it must have been a humiliating experience for Yahweh's prophet. It is ironic that this righteous man had to suffer punishment when it was the unrighteousness of the people against which Yahweh has sent him to preach. Again, Jeremiah is vindicated by Yahweh, but notice his perseverence. He could have easily given up after these incidents of persecution, yet he remained faithful.

A final incident that illustrates his strong character and dedication is found in 38:6-13. Jeremiah is thrown into a muddy cistern to die for his messages. It was the ultimate insult. Instead of being honored for his preaching, he was considered no better than garbage to be tossed into a muddy hole. One can well imagine the feeling of hopelessness he must have experienced. Again, Yahweh delivers him by sending someone to rescue him, Ebed-melech. But it was not one of his Jewish brethren. Rather, it was a despised foreigner, an Ethiopian. It seems as though even foreigners recognized Yahweh's man and messages, while these rebellious Hebrews could not and would not.

An ordinary man could not have endured such suffering for his cause, regardless of how noble. Yet Jeremiah was obviously no ordinary man. His life serves as a marvelous example of all the finer qualities of humankind, even in the heat of unusually hard circumstances.

But it is Jeremiah's preaching that has so wonderfully convicted and inspired people for long. In fact, at the very root of the word that designated a prophet of the Old Testament, "nabhi", is the idea of speaking forth a message.[3] Jeremiah takes this gift of speaking and raises its quality to new heights of excellence. One cannot help but be impressed by his descriptive phrases and startling imagery. Notice how he ridicules idols:

6

> "Like a scarecrow in a cucumber
>   field are they,
> And they cannot speak;
> They must be carried,
> Because they cannot walk!
> Do not fear them,
> For they can do no harm,
> Nor can they do any good."[4]
>
>   (10:5)

Notice, also, the beauty of this conclusion
to one of his sermons on the coming judgment
of Yahweh for the rebellion and unfaithfulness of Judah. It could stand alone as a
credo of the faith of Yahweh:

> Thus says the Lord, "Let not a
> wise man boast of his wisdom,
> and let not the mighty man boast
> of his might, let not a rich man
> boast of his riches; but let him
> who boasts boast of this, that
> he understands and knows Me, that
> I am the Lord who exercises loving
> kindness, justice, and righteous-
> ness on earth; for I delight in
> these things," declares the Lord.
> (9:23,24)

Finally, one needs also to appreciate
just how far he carried the images portrayed
in his messages. He often acted out his messages to illustrate his point. This writer
has chosen to call these incidents "enacted
parables", but they are sometimes called
"symbolic acts". There are usually three
parts to each: the command by Yahweh to do
the act, the performance of the act by the
prophet, and the interpretation of the act
by Yahweh through the prophet (for a complete
list of the enacted parables of Jeremiah see
the appendix).

Much could also be said about his fierce
denunciations of the incompetent leadership
and false prophets of his day (22,23), as well

7

as his foresight in seeing the decay and eventual collapse of his once proud and powerful country. His was a loud voice crying in the wilderness of the political and religious chaos of his day. It was to a people who "excelled in deeds of wickedness" (5:28) that Jeremiah spoke his brave sermons of repentance, judgment, and eventual restoration. His own words describe his mission in life, as well as his struggle. He was a man of words, and oh how those words wrenched from his soul like sparks of fire:

> "For each time I speak I cry aloud;
> I proclaim violence and destruction,
> Because for me the word of the Lord
>   has resulted
> In reproach and derision all day long.
> But if I say, 'I will not remember
>   Him
> Or speak any more in His name,'
> Then in my heart it becomes like a
>   burning fire
> Shut up in my bones;
> And I am weary of holding it in,
> And I cannot endure it."
>   (20:8,9)

The reader is deeply indebted to Jeremiah's personal scribe, Baruch, who faithfully wrote the messages of Jeremiah (36:4). It is to his credit and our benefit that, except for a humiliating experience given in Chapter 45, he does not intrude his own thoughts or personality into this work. Certainly his association with Jeremiah, who was ostracized by his society, cost him much personal gain as an educated man. Yet because of his commitment to Jeremiah he gained greater fame than he could have otherwise, plus Yahweh, Himself, protected him when judgment and disaster struck (45:5).

NOTES

[1] For another possibility see John Bright, _A History of Israel_ (Philadelphia: The West-minister Press, 1974), pp. LXXXVII, LXXXVIII.

[2] A. W. Strange, _The Cambridge Bible for Schools and Colleges: The Book of the Prophet Jeremiah Together with Lamentations_, ed. J. J. S. Perowne (Cambridge: Cambridge University Press, 1887), pg. X.

[3] E. J. Young, _My Servants the Prophets_ (Grand Rapids: Wm. B. Erdmans Publishing Co., 1978), pg. 58.

[4] All scripture quotes are from the New American Standard Bible, The Lockman Foundation (LaHabra, California: Foundation Press Publications, 1971).

II. <u>Jeremiah, His Times</u>

Jeremiah's messages cannot be divorced from the time in which he gave them. The focal point of all that he spoke was both the religious and political crises of Judah in the late seventh and early sixth centuries B.C.

The very roots of Judah's problems lay in the distant past. Solomon set the tone of religious thought for the next four hundred years by his acceptance of and encouragement in pagan worship. Because of the alliances he made with foreign countries, he married many different women of these countries. They brought with them to Jerusalem their pagan religions. I Kings 10 lists the different nations with which Solomon made alliances and the various gods of those countries for which Solomon erected temples. The author of I Kings says this "turned his heart away" from Yahweh (I Kings 10:3). Given the example of this great king worshipping idols, plus the fact that he forced the people to pay for and help erect these pagan temples it is no wonder the people began to regularly practice idolatry.

In the tenth century B.C. the vast building projects of Solomon called for heavy taxation and Hebrew slave labor. This oppression of the common people finally led to the rebellion of the ten northern tribes of Israel at the death of Solomon. The kingdom of Israel was thus divided into two separate countries; Israel, the Northern Kingdom, was ruled by Rehoboam; Judah, the Southern Kingdom, was ruled by Jeroboam.

Because the Hebrew people had been taught for years to center their religious practice around the Temple at Jerusalem in Judah, Jero-

boam had to think of a way to keep his people
from going to Jerusalem to worship, thus,
opening the possibility of the reunification
of the nation. This he accomplished by set-
ting up his own religion of two golden calves.
One was at Bethel, a very famous place honored because of their ancestor Jacob and his
encounter with God there. The other golden
calf was put in Dan, the farthest geographi-
cal point in Israel away from Jerusalem.

The nations then lived apart for about
two hundred years. They fought their own
wars, and sometimes even fought each other.
Although they each were weakened by this split,
they managed to maintain their independence
for about one hundred years.

In the mid-ninth century B.C. Assyria began its rise to power, testing its neighbors
to the west. Because of problems in Assyria
its armies were not able to withstand a coalition of kings in Palestine. This brought a
short period of prosperity to Palestine. During this time all sorts of immoralities and
injustices were common practice among the people
of Israel, the Northern Kingdom. Both Amos and
Hosea record some of these problems, and both
spoke out boldly against them. The book of
Amos reveals a startling example of the inhumanity of the times:

> "... they sell the righteous for
>   money
> And the needy for a pair of sandals.
> These who pant after the very dust
>   of the earth
> On the heads of the helpless
> Also turn aside the way of the
>   humble;
> And a man and his father resort to
>   the same girl..."
>   (Amos 2:6,7)

Also during this time idolatry was common-

12

place. The golden calves have already been mentioned as the national religion of the Northern Kingdom. They also worshipped the ancient god and goddesses of the ancient Canaanites--Baal, Asherah, and Ashtareth. The religions called for debasing practices such as sacred prostitution and homosexuality.[1] The prophets Amos and Hosea both saw the possibility of the return of Assyria to carry away Israel into captivity. This was to be God's judgment for the inhumanity and idolatry of the time (Hosea 10:5,6).

After the death of Jeroboam II Israel degenerated into a state of near anarchy. The oppression and injustice described by Amos may have contributed to the political chaos. After Jeroboam's death there was a quick succession of five kings in Israel, each gaining control by murder or intrigue, finally ending when Pekah gained control. As Assyria focused its attention westward, the nations in its path grouped into the same coalition of the ninth century that had repelled the Assyrian invasion then. But Ahaz, king of Judah, was unwilling to join this coalition. This led to the invasion of Judah by the coalition, hoping to force Judah into joining them. Ahaz frantically appealed to Assyria for help, despite the objections of Isaiah the prophet (Is. 7:1-8:18). Assyria accepted Judah's plea for help, and invaded and destroyed the Northern Kingdom of Israel.

Judah's appeal to Assyria was to cost it dearly. Even though Judah was saved from the coalition of neighboring countries, it still had to pay tribute to Assyria and in effect, became a vassal state of Assyria.[2] It had escaped the complete destruction experienced by Israel, but was by no means free. Along with paying tribute to Assyria Judah also had to recognize Assyria's gods. There was even a pagan altar built in the Temple of Yahweh in Jerusalem (II Kings 16:10-15). But Judah was spared loss of territory.

Although Judah became a vassal-state of Assyria, it does not mean the people readily accepted this fate. After the death of Ahaz, Hezekiah became king and instituted various religious reforms. Perhaps his religious reforms reflected the desire of many in Judah to be free of Assyrian domination as represented by their gods in Jerusalem. This open display of rebellion toward Assyria soon brought its army back to Judah. Hezekiah had refused to pay tribute (II Kings 18:7), but when besieged by a large army, he surrendered and gave the Assyrians a large amount of silver and gold (II Kings 18:14-16).[3]

The Assyrians returned some time later to subject Judah, take its people into captivity, and get more of the same treasures taken earlier. The army besieged Jerusalem and shouted taunts and threats at Hezekiah. Hezekiah's response was humiliation before and prayer to Yahweh. Yahweh's response came through the prophet Isaiah. It was a promise of deliverance.

Judah was again saved from loss of territory by some kind of miraculous intervention (II Kings 19), but, again were not free from Assyrian domination. Soon after the incident of II Kings 19, Hezekiah died and was replaced by his son Manasseh, who was strongly pro-Assyrian.

Manasseh reestablished close political ties with Assyria. He also reinstated Assyrian religious practices in the Temple in Jerusalem. Along with these pagan practices, he also established the ancient Canaanite religions with their gross immoralities, and cancelled all of Hezekiah's religious reforms. The scriptures record that he even began the practice of child sacrifice to the god Moloch (II Kings 21:6, 23:10).[4]

It was during the reign of Manasseh that

14

the pagan practices of Jeremiah's day had become firmly entrenched. Jeremiah was to later
say concerning this polytheism:

> "But where are your gods
> Which you made for yourself?
> Let them arise, if they can
>   save you
> In the time of your trouble;
> For according to the number
>   of your cities
> Are your gods, O Judah."
>   (2:28)

Manasseh continued his evil practices
and allegiance to Assyria throughout his reign.
When he died in 642 B.C. his son Amon ruled.
For two years he, too, carried on the tradition
of his father until he was assassinated. A
group of landowners then executed the assassins
(II Kings 21:24), and placed Amon's son,
Josiah, on the throne; he was only eight years
old.

During the reign of Josiah, Assyria began
its general decline until it was finally destroyed in 612 B.C. The fall of Assyria was
due to attacks by barbarous tribes to its
north and, later, a powerful coalition of Medes
and Babylonians. It was this alliance of
Babylon and Media under the leadership of
Nabopolassar that was to spell Assyria's final
defeat. These allies besieged and destroyed
Nineveh, Assyria's capital city, in 612 B.C.,
and the survivors fled to Egypt.

Essentially, then, Judah had once again
gained its independence. Assyria could no
longer control its outlying vassal states so
they were free to seek their own destiny. As
a way of expressing that independence Josiah
began a large-scale religious reform to purge
Judah of all vestiges of foreign domination,
namely, the gods of Assyria which represented
the nation itself. When the book of the Law

15

was discovered in a wall of the Temple during its repairs, it gave new impetus and meaning to the reform. Since ancient governments were inextricably interwoven with their religion(s), it is correct to note that the religious reform was a reflection of the nation's political independence.

In the midst of this reform Jeremiah began his ministry. In fact, the prophet Zephaniah and he are credited with playing an important role in the implementation of Josiah's reform through their preaching.[5] But the kind of lasting reform hoped for by the prophets never materialized.

Because Josiah had extended his reform to the territory of Israel, the people there had no local shrines at which to worship; Josiah had destroyed them and had localized worship in Jerusalem. But because many were unwilling to travel to Jerusalem to worship, or were scorned as less than equal persons by the Jews there, there was a secularization of the society. Also, since religion was localized in Jerusalem, the priests there developed a spirit of elitism which effectively alienated many who were not a part of their ranks. On the surface the reform looked good, but it did not effectively deal with the moral depravity of the populace.

So while the reform of Josiah did much to alleviate the moral and spiritual decay of Judah, it also ushered in a time of a general feeling of security since the external requirements of the Mosaic Law had been satisfied. But the sins of society had not been checked, and it was this hypocrisy that eventually led to Judah's downfall (7:8-10). In fact, the pride with which the leaders regarded their obtaining and knowledge of the Law caused them to no longer regard the prophetic word (8:4-9).

The sense of security stemmed from the way the religious leaders interpreted the Law of Moses. They thought that external compliance with Yahweh's Law would obligate Him to protect them, their Temple, and their land. The Temple of Yahweh became the super- stitious symbol of safety. Since they be- lieved Yahweh lived there, then as long as they kept it in good physical shape and wor- shipped there, at least perfunctorily, Yah- weh had to preserve them (7:4). Jeremiah tried to warn them that it is internal com- pliance with the Law of Moses, a change of one's heart or inner disposition, that would bring Yahweh's blessing (7:5-7). But Judah would not respond to his plea (7:13,14).

During this time Babylon was continuing its rise to power. As the Babylonian's dom- inance in Palestine began to effect the area, Egypt tried to break its hold there by trying to push the Babylonians out of Haran. When the Egyptians under Neco II pushed north Josiah tried to stop them. It is not known if he was afraid of Egyptian domination or was an ally of Babylon. In either case he was the loser because Neco II and his army defeated Josiah and his troops at Megiddo in 609 B.C. Josiah was killed and his son, Jehoahaz reigned in his place.

After reigning only three months Jeho- ahaz was deposed, deported to Egypt, and his brother Elakim put in his place. (His name was changed to Jehoiakim). Judah became a vassal state of Egypt, forced to pay a heavy tribute.

Under Jehoiakim the reform of Josiah failed, and there was a return to the pagan practices of the past. Also, Jehoiakim proved to be a petty tyrant concerned only for him- self, (22:13-19) and was completely calloused to Jeremiah's preaching (Chp. 36). In fact, prophets who spoke out against the status quo

17

were imprisoned or killed (26:20-23). Even
Jeremiah was threatened (36:26).

The Egyptian dominance of Judah continued
until the Egyptian forces were defeated at the
battle of Charchemish in 605 B.C. by Babylon.
Although Babylon did not come up against Judah,
Jehoiakim gave his support to its leader,
Nebuchadnezzar (II Kings 24:1). Many leaders
of Judah were taken to serve in Babylon among
whom was Daniel and his three friends. Jehoiakim
did this for three years until Egypt began another attempt to oust the Babylonians from Palestine in 601 B.C. Although neither side won,
Jehoiakim was optimistic enough about his chan-
ces against Babylon to rebel.

But Jehoiakim's rebellion was short lived.
Nebuchadnezzar sent mercenaries to keep Judah
off-balance while he regrouped his forces
(II Kings 24:2). In 598 B.C. Nebuchadnezzar
besieged Jerusalem. During the siege Jehoiakim
died and was replaced by his son Jeconiah (also
known as Jehoiachin). After three months
Jehoiachin surrendered the city. The leaders
of the government, the leading citizens, and
an enormous amount of booty was taken to Babylon (II Kings 24:13,14). Ezekiel the priest/
prophet was probably taken with this group.
The king's uncle Mattaniah (also known as Zedekiah) was placed on the throne and reigned from
598 B.C. to 586 B.C.

One would think that the strength of the
Babylonian army would have humbled Judah, especially in the light of the humiliating take-
over of Jerusalem in 598 B.C. But Judah was
terribly stubborn. During the next ten years
Judah was constantly agitating Babylon and
trying to form a coalition with other countries
to defeat it (27:1-3). Jeremiah tried again
to warn Judah of the consequences of its
actions (27:8), but, again, it was to no avail.

By 588 B.C. Judah was confident enough to

rebel again, hoping that other nations would join forces with it against Babylon. But these allies did not join them. In fact, the ones who did not remain neutral joined forces with the Babylonians (Psalms 137:7) in defeating them.

Babylon moved quickly against the insurgents and, again, besieged Jerusalem in 588 B.C. The city bravely held out until 586 B.C., when Zedekiah tried to break out to safety. He was captured and forced to watch his family being killed before his eyes were put out. He was then taken in captivity to Babylon with most of Judah (II Kings 25:7). In his place the Babylonians named Gedaliah as governor of the now Babylonian province of Judah.

All during these times of political and spiritual crises Jeremiah was preaching his messages of repentance, judgment, obedience, and eventual restoration. His words fell on deaf ears (5:21). It was a time of fierce nationalism that would tolerate no message of humility, either before Yahweh or a foreign government. Immorality and injustice were the common practices (9:4-6); the leaders and their people seemed to care only for themselves (8:10).

In this hostile climate it was no easy task for this man to speak out for truth and morality. Yet Jeremiah did so with great fervor and great personal courage. If the tide of evil was at its crest, then he would be the bulwark of righteousness to stand against it.

Notes

[1] John Bright, A History of Israel (Philadelphia: The Westminister Press, 1974), pp.
116, 117.

[2] For an ancient depiction of tribute-
paying of a Hebrew king to a foreign power
see D.J. Wiseman, Illustrations from Biblical
Archaeology (Grand Rapids: Wm. B. Erdmans
Publishing Co., 1958), pp 5-7.

[3] Ibid. pg 60

[4] J. A. Thompson, The New International
Commentary on the Old Testament: The Book of
Jeremiah (Grand Rapids: Wm. B. Erdmans Pub-
lishing Co., 1980), pg. 13.

[5] Bright, A History of Israel, pp. 319, 320.

"...'Return faithless Israel,' declares the Lord; 'I will not look
upon you in anger. For I am gra-
cious,' declares the Lord;...'"
3:12

III. Repentance

This message of repentance is a recurring
thought throughout Jeremiah's preaching, although the focus here will be on chapters three
and four. As previously noted the nation of
Judah was totally immersed in injustice, immorality, and idolatry. It is no wonder, then,
that this message would serve as Jeremiah's
main theme in his preaching to these people.

It is interesting to note that Jeremiah
uses a clever play-on-words in describing Judah's disobedience. God sends him to proclaim
a message, in the hearing of the people of Judah, northward to the people of Israel who had
been taken into captivity by the Assyrians over
one hundred years earlier. It was a message
calling for Israel's repentance, but it was
clearly intended for the people of Judah. The
word used in 3:12 is "repent" or "return"; it
literally means "turn back". The next word
in the text is "faithless" or "backsliding";
it literally means "back turning", and is
clearly a play-on-words to emphasize the point.
So Jeremiah is saying "Turn back, back-turning
Israel (Judah)", thus both characterizing
their disobedient tendencies and exhorting
them to right behavior before God.

Repentance is a fascinating concept because of all that is implicit in its practice.
First of all, it means to turn away from rebellion or disobedience to God. The idea is
that one completely forsakes his disobedience

and returns to a complete devotion to God. Jeremiah senses that the reform of Josiah did not accomplish true repentance because he says "... Judah... did not return to Me (Yahweh) with all her heart..."(3:10). But one cannot truly repent unless he knows what is the correct standard of right behavior and what he must do to arrive at that place. So then, besides the idea of turning back, there is also implied that one's turn-about is based on the standard of behavior established in the Law of Moses. When Jeremiah says "... you have not obeyed My (Yahweh's) voice..." (3:13), it probably refers to the Law of God recorded in the Pentateuch, the first five books of the Old Testament. And when one realizes he needs to repent he must do so by "... acknowledging your iniquity, that you have transgressed against the Lord your God..." (3:13).

The final step in true repentance involved complete submission to Yahweh as a son to his father. "... You shall call Me (Yahweh), My Father, and not turn away from following Me" (3:19).

But it is quite evident from history that the Hebrew people wanted nothing to do with Yahweh, His Law, or His prophets. Jeremiah refers to this sordid history of God's people by the use of a graphic illustration in 3:1-14. It is reminiscent of the analogy used by the prophet Hosea. Yahweh is pictured as a loving husband, and His people are pictured as an adulterous wife. The "adultery" referred to was the desire of the Hebrews to look to foreign nations for guidance and help rather than Yahweh (3:2). These people also accepted the immoral pagan practices of these foreign nations (3:6). ("Under every green tree..." in 3:6 refers to the immoral worship practices associated with the Syrian goddess Asherah.) The Hebrews have become so ingrained with this "adultery" that they are called "harlot(s)". Jeremiah cannot understand this terribly rebellious condition of his nation. He expresses God's incredulity at the situation, "And I thought, 'After she has done all these things, she will return to Me'; but she did not return..." (3:7). The word, again, used here is the word that means "turn back" (Shuv-Hebrew). (In fact, the word is used eight times in 3:1-4:4). Yahweh looked for repentance in His people, but did not find it.

Jeremiah then sounds a severe warning to Judah for this unwillingness to repent. He continues his reference to Israel, the Northern Kingdom, as an example of Yahweh's dealings with the unrepentant. He describes Yahweh's judgment of Israel as a "divorce" (3:8). The "sending away" of divorce is an obvious reference to the Assyrian captivity to which the people of Israel were sent. Despite this graphic lesson of history the people of Judah were not impressed. In fact, the people of Judah are said to have regarded their immoralities as being insignificant (3:9).

Given this brazen attitude of Judah concerning their sin, it is no wonder Jeremiah so adamantly calls for true repentance. If Yahweh sent Israel into captivity for similar action and attitude, then Judah will receive the same judgment.

Jeremiah then explains the evidence of true repentance in 4:1,2. The first part involved ridding themselves of the objects of their rebellion. Throughout his preaching Jeremiah strongly denounces the practice of idolatry. If true repentance meant following the Law of Moses then at the very heart of that Law was the need for complete devotion to the Law - Giver, Yahweh. Yahweh was to be set-off from every other object of worship. Yahweh demanded complete allegiance from His people. To worship anything or anyone else was tantamount to treason.

23

There are many places in which Jeremiah contemptuously contrasts the lifelessness of an idol to the majesty and glory of Yahweh-God. But there is no denunciation of idolatry so sarcastic as is found in 10:1-16. Here we see that an idol cannot walk, speak, or do anything, whereas Yahweh is the great Creator of Heaven and earth, the One who controls all the elements, and the One worthy of all reverence. This is reminiscent of other prophets' messages, Hosea 9:10, Isaiah 44:9-23, Habakkuk 2. Also, Ezekiel, who prophesied during the latter part of Jeremiah's ministry, describes just how far these people of Judah had gone with their idolatry. He sees the idolatry of Judah even in the Temple of Yahweh (Ezekiel 8:3). It is described as an "idol of jealousy" because Yahweh was jealous for the devotion of His people. This is the whole point of their need for repentance.

The first way, then, these people can demonstrate true repentance is to completely destroy all forms of idolatry from their midst.

The other way the people were to demonstrate true repentance was to alter their behavior to conform to the standards of Yahweh (4:2). The clear implication here is that one may swear "As the Lord lives" only if he were in fellowship with Yahweh. The "truth", "justice", and "righteousness" listed are attributes of Yahweh and are the qualities for which one is to strive if he would live in fellowship with Him.

The demonstration of true repentance described in 4:1,2 would greatly benefit the people of Judah, but it would also have far reaching effects. The nations would discover that the attendant blessings of Yahweh for true repentance were of such enjoyment that they, too, would surrender to the sovereignty of Yahweh. The example of Judah's submission and subsequent enjoyment of the blessings of the covenant of Yahweh would have a tremendous effect on the behavior of the world.

True repentance involved three main actions. First, the people were to change their attitude and "turn back" to Yahweh from their rebellious ways. Next, they were to destroy all symbols of their disobedience by destroying all forms of idolatry. Finally, they were to demonstrate their repentance by altering their behavior to comply with the attributes of Yahweh as revealed in His Law.

In proclaiming the message of repentance Jeremiah never fails to mention these qualifying actions. He saw it as the only way Yahweh would once again accept these people in fellowship and give them His blessing.

> "'Why should I pardon you?
> Your sons have forsaken Me
> And sworn by those who are not gods...
> Shall I not punish these people?'
>   declares the Lord..."
>   5:7,9a

IV. Judgment

At the end of his sermon on repentance in
chapter four Jeremiah has begun to imply Yahweh's coming judgment. He begins his description of this destruction by comparing it to
a storm:

> "... the mountains ... were quaking,
> And all the hills moved to and fro.
> ... all the birds of the heavens had
>   fled.
> ... the fruitful land was a wilder-
>   ness,
> And all the cities were pulled down
> Before the Lord, before His fierce
>   anger."
>   4:24-26

He goes on to describe the desolation that will
follow such judgment, and he begins to hint that
the "storm" that will cause this will be an
invading army (4:29).

In this long section on the judgment of
Judah by Yahweh, 4:23-6:30, Jeremiah gradually
reveals Yahweh's intention of sending an army
against Judah as punishment, and, by degrees,
describes that army. But what is very interesting is that throughout this condemnation
Jeremiah repeatedly shows Judah exactly why
this judgment is coming. This alternating move-
ment from judgment to sin is very effective in
emphasizing both the impact of Judah's apostasy

27

on Yahweh and Yahweh's justification for His
action against them.

One can see in this sermon a terrible
description of destruction. But one can also
gain important insights into the character of
Yahweh. Throughout the Old Testament He is
variously represented as the great Creator,
Sovereign Lord, Almighty God, etc. If there
were anyone who did not have to justify His
actions it would be Yahweh. Yet He graciously
condescends to tell His sinful people exactly
why He is punishing them. Here are some of
the reasons given:

> "Your ways and your deeds
> Have brought these things to you...
> > 4:18

> "... they are shrewd to do evil,
> But to do good they do not know."
> > 4:22

> "... they have refused to take
>   correction...
> they have refused to repent."
> > 5:3

> "... they also excell in deeds of
>   wickedness;..."
> > 5:28

> "... everyone is greedy for gain;..."
> > 6:13

If anyone were to question Yahweh's motives
the overwhelming evidence given would silence
him. In His mercy He has shown them exactly
why He is punishing them.

Another important insight into the character of Yahweh inferred here is His absolute
justice. One might argue that Yahweh was actually holding Judah "to the letter of the Law".
While this is true one must also remember that
His longsuffereing love and mercy had kept them

28

on "probation" for several hundred years. Yahweh had withheld His judgment in hopes that Judah would repent. In fact, Yahweh had sent His many prophets to various generations of these people and had not seen any lasting change in their rebellious attitude. Jeremiah says this about Judah's regard for the word of Yahweh:

"To whom shall I speak and give
   warning
That they may hear?
Behold, their ears are closed,
And they cannot listen.
Behold, the word of the Lord has
   become a reproach to them;
They have no delight in it." 6:10

Yahweh is justified in His judgment because of the standard He had set for His people. That standard by which His people were measured was His Law. This was established in the wilderness under the leadership of Moses when Yahweh brought them from Egypt to the promised land, Palestine. The covenant made in the wilderness was for that generation and each succeeding generation in that Moses commanded the people to teach their children Yahweh's Law (Deut. 4:10). It was this Law that justified Yahweh's judgment. Years before Moses had said that part of the punishment for continued disobedience to the Law would be a siege, invasion, and destruction by a hostile power (Deut. 28:49-57). Jeremiah is referring to just that section of the Law when he warns of impending doom at the hands of an enemy. In fact, he almost quotes directly from the Law in 5:15.

The Old Testament concept of the Law was inherently bound up within the nature of Yahweh.[1] Yahweh's actions were naturally legal -- He rewarded righteousness and punished evildoing. Jeremiah even saw nature as within the bounds of Yahweh's legal system:

29

> "... I have placed the sand as
>   a boundary for the sea
> An eternal decree, so it cannot
>   cross-over it."
>   5:22

He uses birds and Yahweh's laws of nature to
emphasize Judah's ignorance of the Law of
Moses:

> "Even the stork in the sky
> Knows her seasons;
> And the turtledove and the
>   swift and the thresh
> Observe the time of their
>   migration;
> But my people do not know
> The ordinance of the Lord."   8:7

Without such a legal system there could
be no strength or force to insure consistent
action either in nature or among humankind.
At the very heart of Yahweh's covenant with
humankind was His system of checks and balances.
Not only did the Old Testament prophets see
this Law as insuring Yahweh's will in the
world, they also saw it as insuring humankind
of a consistent perception of the nature of
Yahweh.   Righteousness and judgment were essential parts of His character; therefore
Yahweh worked by the method of Law (Jer. 9:24).
But Judah refused to heed it; "... as for My
Law, they have rejected it also" (6:19).

As did many other prophets, Jeremiah
shows Judah the cause-effect reaction of the
Law.   The sins of Judah, or the cause, have
already been listed.   The effect will be "a
great destruction" (6:1).   This cause-effect
result of the Law was not an impersonal show
of force.   Rather, Jeremiah clearly reflects
the anguish of Yahweh in bringing about the
circumstance of judgment:

> "My sorrow is beyond healing

30

My heart is faint within me!
Behold, listen! The cry of the
    daughter of my people from a
    distant land:
'Is the Lord not in Zion? Is her
    king not within her?'
Why have they provoked Me with
    their graven images, with
    foreign idols?" 8:18,19

Jeremiah thus shows that Yahweh is both
merciful and just in that Yahweh has conde-
scended to reveal the motive of His judgment,
Judah's sin, and the justification for His
judgment, His own Law.

The fierce enemy to come against Judah
was Babylon under Nebuchadnezzar. In fact,
Jeremiah calls Nebuchadnezzar Yahweh's servant
(27:6). Jeremiah sees him and his army as the
fulfillment of his prediction of judgment. In
his first "vision" or "prophetic consciousness"
he "saw" an invading army from the general
direction of Babylon, north, marching to destroy
Jerusalem. He again alludes to a "northern"
power several times in this section (6:1,22).

Jeremiah describes the terrible destruction
that will come. He lists day and night attacks
(6:4,5), a siege (6:6), sickness and disease
(6:7), great cruelty (6:23), abject terror (6:23),
"devouring" of people, cities, and homes (5:15-
17). This is almost exactly what archaeologi-
cal evidence has shown to have happened.[2] Almost all of the cities of Judah were razed, many
people died in battle or of starvation and disease, and many others were deported to Babylon.
All normal life was completely disrupted, the
center of their religion was gone (the Temple was
completely destroyed), and whole families were
either killed or separated by flight or deportation. It was a very sad time in the history of
Israel, but it is even more tragic when one
realizes all of this could have been avoided if
only the people had turned to Yahweh:

"Wash your heart from evil, O
    Jerusalem
That you may be saved..."   4:14

Notes

[1] Leon Morris, The Apostolic Preaching of the Cross (Grand Rapids: Wm. B. Erdman Publishing Co., 1980), pp. 253-258.

[2] John Bright, A History of Israel (Philadelphia: The Westminister Press, 1974), pp. 344,345.

"And you shall say to them, 'This
is the nation that did not obey the
voice of the Lord their God or accept correction; truth has perished
and has been cut off from their
mouth.'"   7:28

V. The Way of Obedience

In chapter seven one can read what is
called by many scholars Jeremiah's "Temple
Sermon". This sermon is meant to both dispel
a pernicious superstition and proclaim the true
way of obedience to Yahweh.

As has already been noted the people of
Judah have for years committed all kinds of
transgressions against the Law of Yahweh. In
doing so they have continually violated the
covenant with Him. The result will be judgment in the form of terrible destruction by
an invading army. But few, if any, were willing to accept the inevitability of judgment
and punishment. Conveniently, the false
prophets developed a peaceful, hopeful message in an attempt to calm any anxiety the
people might have concerning the Babylonians'
rise to power.

The false message of peace and security
developed by the false prophets incorporated
a superstition about the Temple of Yahweh.
In 7:4 it is obvious the people had been en-
couraged to invoke the name of the Temple in
an almost magical way to insure the protection
of Jerusalem.[1] Their argument was that since
Yahweh had chosen Jerusalem as His city
(Psalms 132:13,14), and the Temple as His
dwelling place (Psalms 11:4), then no harm
would befall it. Indeed, a supernatural deliverance of Jerusalem had occurred in the

past during the reign of Hezekiah that would have strengthened this superstition about Jerusalem and the Temple (see the account of Yahweh's defeat of the Assyrians in II Kings 18:17-19:36).

Jeremiah uses a very graphic illustration to show this superstition to be completely false. He points in the direction of the ruins of Shiloh. It was at Shiloh that the Tabernacle of the wilderness had been erected when the people first possessed the promised land. Although there is no record of who destroyed Shiloh nor how it was done, the clear implication is that destruction came because of the "wickedness" (7:12) of Israel. One can read of this "wickedness" of idolatry, murder, and rape in Judges 18 - I Samuel 4.

The prophet, then, is showing that Yahweh was under no obligation to guarantee the inviolablity of Jerusalem or the Temple at the expense of obedience to His Law. The prophet clearly respected Yahweh, His Law, and the need for sacrifice. But he knew all was futile if there were no compliance with Yahweh's commands. The people were to trust in and obey Yahweh, not the building built to honor Him.

It is entirely appropriate that Jeremiah is sent to the Temple to proclaim this message (7:12). The force of his words would have struck home to the worshipper entering the building to offer sacrifice to Yahweh. The words of 7:21-26 were especially solemn, given Israel's history of perfunctory religion. Their religion was not to be only external sacrifice, but was to be "internalized" in an attitude of obedience to the Law and the prophets (7:25).

If there were any question as to the certainty of Yahweh's judgment for their disobedience, Jeremiah answers that with another illustration (7:14). A little over 150 years earlier Judah's neighbors, their "brothers" of the Northern Kingdom, had been sent into captivity by Yahweh. In 722-21 B.C. the Assyrian army overran the country, destroying its cities and land. In recording this event the author of II Kings (17:7-18) gives a long list of sins of the Northern Kingdom as the reason for its destruction and deportation of its people. Jeremiah is saying Judah, too, will suffer a similar fate (at the hands of the Babylonian army) for the same kinds of sins.

In contrast to these blatant acts of disobedience Jeremiah presents a very clear picture of what it would take to obey Yahweh. If a person in that society had become so steeped in paganism as to no longer know the correct way, then the prophet was going to instruct him.

To the prophet obedience meant practicing justice between persons and no longer practicing idolatry (7:5-7). Justice meant they should help one person to his rights against another.[2]

Since the Law pronounced punishment on those who opposed the weak (Ex. 22:21; Deut. 24:17; 27:19) then those who delivered or helped the same were considered obedient. It was essential to the covenant that these demands were met. In the covenant a Hebrew's first response was to Yahweh; his second response was to his fellow human. Since the first response had been broken by idolatry, it was inevitable the second response would result in injustice.

The Law clearly stated why the people were to obey in doing this (Deut. 24:19-22). They were to emulate their Benefactor, Yahweh, in their actions. Worship of Yahweh involved sacrifice and praise, but it also involved a practical demonstration of their beliefs. If they were to belong to Yahweh then they were to act as He had acted in kindness, mercy, and justice. This action would set them apart from the other nations and show them to be truly covenant people.

It is tragic to note, however, the people's rebellious response. It seems as though in response to his preaching there was no repentance or right behavior:

Message	Response
vs. 4 Don't trust in... the temple	vs. 10,11 They stood in the Temple – their supposed protection – and proclaimed His deliverance
vs. 6a Don't oppress: alien, orphan, widow	vs. 9a they stole, committed adultery, and swore falsely
vs. 6b Don't shed innocent blood	vs. 9a they committed murder
vs. 6c Don't walk after other gods	vs. 9b they offered sacrifice to Baal and walked after other gods.

Their disobedience is so complete that Yahweh even prohibits prayer for them. This seemed to be the final seal of their rejection. Not only were they completely given over to sin, but they were even beyond the intercession of Yahweh's servant. Even though he had proclaimed repentance, the possibility of the people's response was so remote as to render intercessory prayer useless. The finality of such a possibility failed to impress them.

In this state of near-apostasy the people's attitude is expressed in the immature actions of a spoiled and rebellious child. Instead of turning to Yahweh in humble obedience they are shown to be deliberately disobedient. When Jeremiah preaches against idolatry they do exactly the opposite. Instead of ceasing from it they do it to "spite" God (7:18). But this "spite" does not affect Yahweh as much as it affects them (7:19).

38

Their attitude and actions have shown
them to be totally disobedient. It led to
the obvious conclusion concerning this rebellion; Jeremiah will speak to them, but they
won't listen (7:27). This has been the history
of their relationship with Yahweh:

> "... they did not obey or incline
> their ear, but walked in their
> own counsels and in the stubborness
> of their evil heart, and went back-
> ward and not forward." (7:24)

Notes

[1] J.A. Thompson, The New International Commentary on the Old Testament: The Book of Jeremiah (Grand Rapids: Wm. B. Erdmans Publishing Co., 1980), pg. 277.

[2] C. F. Keil, Commentary on the Old Testament: Jeremiah, Lamentations (Grand Rapids: Wm. B. Erdmans Publishing Co., 1978), pg. 154.

"Thus says the Lord, the God of Israel,
'Write all the words which I have spoken
to you in a book.
   For, behold, days are coming,' declares
the Lord, 'when I will restore the fortunes
of My people Israel and Judah.'..."

30:2,3a

VI. Restoration

Judah was in one of the worst crises of
its history. Many of the people were involved
in all kinds of injustice and oppression against
their very own (2:34; 5:26-31; 7:4-11). They
were also continually giving themselves over
to various pagan deities, and indulging in all
kinds of debasing immoral practices (2:26-28;
5:7-9; 7:17,18). But the worst and most tragic
fact was that the people were going to suffer
the harsh judgment of Yahweh for these transgressions (4:5-8,14-18; 5:7-9). Babylon was
about to destroy them!

For years many prophets had been sent to
proclaim repentance to Judah: Micah, Isaiah,
Habakkuk, Zephaniah, Jeremiah, and Ezekiel.
There had been no lasting change and the patience
of Yahweh had run its course. Yet there was
"not... (to be) ... a complete destruction" (5:18).
There was a glimmer of hope.

Among the prophets of Judah, Jeremiah
stands out in many respects as one of the
greatest. This can be seen in his life and
preaching, but his greatness is especially evident in his words of hope to a doomed nation.
Throughout his ministry no prophet had more
strongly denounced the sins of Judah than Jeremiah. He also very graphically and forcefully
described the terrible punishment of Yahweh for
these numerous transgressions; however, inter-
spersed throughout his preaching one can find

a hint of a future restoration (3:12-19; 4:1,2,27; 5:18; 16:14,15; 29:11-14; 30-33).

The best and most complete description of Yahweh's plan of restoration is found in chapters 30-33. This section is a collection of Jeremiah's many years of prophecies of hope, probably edited by his own hand.[1] This section was given in the tenth year of Zedekiah's reign, about 587, 86 B.C.[2] Jerusalem was in the throes of its worst siege by the Babylonians and was about to fall.[3] When Jerusalem was totally surrounded by the very army he had prophesied would come as an instrument of Yahweh's anger, Jeremiah did not gloat over his prophetic accuracy. Rather, he saw beyond the immediate crisis to a time when the people of Yahweh would be recipients of His mercy and not his anger. This section is appropriately called by most commentators "The Book of Consolation" (or comfort) (30:1-3).

In the midst of this turmoil of fighting, deprivation, frustration, and fear in the siege, Yahweh gives Jeremiah a strange command. He was to buy a field near Jerusalem (32:6,7)! This is incredible when one realizes that the land was worthless since it was about to become Babylonian occupied territory. But this purchase was to be an enacted parable of the mercy of Yahweh. It was meant to illustrate the great truth of a future restoration (32:15). Yahweh had promised release from captivity after seventy years (29:10). Never more than in the present situation did these people need reassurance that there was hope. Even the great prophet who spoke this word of hope was a bit skeptical. Yahweh gave beautiful words of encouragement to this doubting servant:

"Behold, I am the Lord, the God of all flesh; is anything too difficult for Me?"
32:27

Concerning the prophet's questions about how this restoration could take place, Yahweh challenged his inquisitive mind:

42

"Call to Me, and I will answer you, and
I will tell you great and mighty things
which you do not know." 33:3

While this "Book of Consolation" is a ray
of light in the darkness of the siege, it is
more a treatise on the future life of all of
Yahweh's covenant people. It is a full description of the fulfillment of Yahweh's prom-
ises concerning deliverance, peace, and spiritual renewal, a welcome word to a people who
either were already suffering in captivity or
were about to enter captivity in Babylon in a
most violent fashion.

The great theme of this section concerns
the spiritual revival of these people. All
were hoping for deliverance from the immediate
oppression of the Babylonian Army, and that
deliverance would eventually come. But Jeremiah dealt more importantly with the root of
their problem which brought about Yahweh's
judgment. The root lay in their evil heart or
spirit (4:14). There had to be an internal
change before their external actions could
become consistently righteous. This was to be
accomplished in the new covenant (31:31-34;
32:40).

The time that this restoration actually
occurred is a matter of dispute. It is obvious
when reading a passage like this the prophet
looked for Yahweh's restoration immediately
after the exile when the exiled community was
allowed to return to Palestine by Cyrus' decree
(Jer. 30:3,18; 32:41-43, Ezra 1:1-4). In fact,
Ezra specifically states that the decree of
Cyrus that gave Palestine back to the people
was a fulfillment of Jeremiah's prophecy (Ezra
1:1). However, when looking at the restored
community from 535 B.C. until the time of
Christ from the view of the history of Ezra,
Nehemiah, Haggai, and Malachi, one cannot find
evidence of the kind of spiritual renewal
described in 31:31-34. In fact, the people fell

43

far short of the prophetic ideal.[4]   There was
a syncretism of beliefs (Ez. 9:11), fearfulness
and distress (Neh. 1:3), various factions following their own self-interests (Neh. 5:1-5),
corruption in high places (Neh. 13:4-9), laxity
in regard to the Law (Neh. 13:15-18), an unwillingness to rebuild the Temple and reestab-
lish the sacrificial system (Hag. 1:1-11), and
a refusal to bring the required offerings to
the Temple (Mal. 3:7-12).

   The only consistent change one notices
in reading the history of the period in the
scriptures is that there was no continued practice of idolatry after the exile. No longer
were pillars, high places, and idols everywhere
as before the exile (2:28). If the exile did
nothing else besides punish them for their sins,
it did effectively eradicate almost all of the
paganism of the past, and its accompanying
immorality.

   If one is to find the fulfillment of this
restoration, he must look both at the immediate
historical context and beyond. It is true that
the people were restored to their homeland by
the decree of Cyrus after seventy years, as
prophesied by Jeremiah (29:10). It is also true
that their "fortunes" (30:3) were restored in
that they had abundant harvests (31:11,12).
But one must look beyond that period of history
for fulfillment of the great spiritual awakening.

   The description of the spiritual renewal
in 31:31-34 involves a contrast between what had
been Yahweh's plan for humankind and his new
plan. The first is called "... the covenant...
with their father... out of the land of Egypt"
(31:32). This speaks of the old covenant given
Moses at Sinai and affecting all generations
until the implementation of the new covenant.
The old covenant (by implication) was one that
was external, and, historically, involved these
aspects: commandments, responsibility of the
worshipper to follow those commandments, ulti-

44

mate failure because there was no inner disposition to cause the worshipper to obey, and judgment by Yahweh for failure to obey. It was because of this failure and subsequent judgment that brought about the new covenant.

By contrast, the new covenant is an inner covenant that involves the old, but goes beyond it. In the new covenant while there are commandments, they are not externally stamped in stone for strict compliance. Rather, the commandments are stamped in the worshipper's heart, and the worshipper is given an inner disposition to obey those commandments. Because the emphasis of the action is on Yahweh, there is true forgiveness and a true knowledge of Yahweh. This new covenant is unlike the old in that no longer would the bulk of the responsibility rest with the worshipper to find some way by himself to obey, but the worshipper could rest in the promise of the responsibility taken by Yahweh to effect this knowledge and forgiveness within him. He still has the responsibility to submit to Yahweh (by placing his trust in Him), but he no longer has to try to gain the favor of Yahweh by animal sacrifice or strict external compliance to the Law. Now he would realize the grace of Yahweh.

The new covenant is very unique in that one cannot find any of the rudimentary elements of the old: festivals, sacrifice, works. How bold and insightful Jeremiah was! This concept of religion was far advanced for the mind-set of the ancients. It is amazing that Jeremiah could envision such a lofty faith and new age in his time period. Restoration would go beyond the immediate circumstances of political freedom and physical prosperity. There was a higher ideal to which Yahweh planned to conform His people, and that was to completely renew them spiritually.

In examining the new covenant one can see some principal characteristics. First, the initiative is going to be with Yahweh. Notice the emphasis on what Yahweh will do in 31:31-34, "I will ..." is repeated time and again. Next, it will be an inward (soul) covenant. The unchanging, eternal law of Yahweh would not be on tablets of stone in an unapproachable ark as were the Law of Moses, but would be placed on the heart of every believer. Also, the new covenant will be with individuals. While it is true Jeremiah is addressing the restoration of the community of Yahweh, the idea of "each man" (31:34) stands out. It is true that when one reads the Old Testament he sees Yahweh dealing with individuals, but usually Yahweh dealt with the nation as a whole. He still speaks here to the restored community, but never had so much emphasis been placed on each person "knowing" Yahweh. Finally, there is the hint of the universality of the new covenant (31:34). "... From the least to the greatest..." is all-inclusive, destroying any idea that a relationship with Yahweh was only for the spiritually elite like Moses, Aaron, or the prophets.

There are two bases for the new covenant. The first and most important is the forgiveness of Yahweh. The implication is the forgiveness of the violation of the first or old covenant. In the old covenant there was the constant reminder of sin through the various animal sacrifices throughout the religious year, constantly reminding the people of their sins and transgressions of the Law. Indeed, their various idolatries, immoralities, and sins of oppression, before the exile come to mind when reading 31:34. It was the very reason for Yahweh's judgment and the exile. In fact, the people had become so fatalistic about their sins that they thought there was no hope for them. This is the reason for the proverb of 31:29. They thought that because of their ancestors' sins and the failure of the sacrificial system to remove those sins they had no escape from judgment; therefore, no one sought after Yahweh. But Jeremiah is

46

presenting a new idea. Each individual will be responsible for his own sins, but each person also can receive Yahweh's permanent forgiveness. No longer would there be constant reminders of sins through continual animal sacrifice, but Yahweh will "... remember their sin no more" (31:34).

The second basis for the new covenant is the special knowledge given the worshipper. In the old covenant the worshipper could not directly approach Yahweh. Direct access to Him was denied. The only avenue to Yahweh was through human mediators. But in the new covenant individuals are assured a special position of honor. Worshippers could personally and individually "know" Him. The word "know" gives the idea of an intimate, personal knowledge between persons wholly committed to one another.[5] The new covenant would break shadowy barriers of prophets, priests, and a Temple veil, and give the worshipper a new intimate relationship with Yahweh. Whereas once these people were rejected as hopelessly disobedient and rebellious (Jer. 6:30), now they would receive Yahweh's acceptance and forgiveness.

If one is to discover the time frame of the institution of the new covenant, he must investigate the New Testament. The New Testament writers clearly saw no complete fulfillment of the prophecies of restoration immediately after the exile. Instead, they saw the inaguration of the new covenant in the ministry of Jesus Christ.

In discovering how the New Testament writers interpreted the new covenant one must examine various writers and incidents. The first and most important is the record of Christ's words given by Mark (14:24), Matthew (26:28), and Luke (22:20). Christ is explaining the elements of Christian communion, and describes the wine (symbolic of His sacrificial death on the cross) as "... the new covenant in My blood" (Luke 22:20).

Christ saw the way to this new relationship with Yahweh in the new covenant only by way of sacrifice. Only by atoning for humankind's sins would they be able to realize this "knowledge" of Yahweh (Matt. 20:28).

The writer to the Hebrews quotes Jeremiah 31:31-34, and says that Christ is the superior mediator of a better (the new) covenant (Heb. 8:6-12). As a superior mediator he had to die only once for the sin of all humankind, whereas in the old covenant the high priest had to offer an annual sacrifice to atone for sin (Heb. 9:24-28). He also says that Christ is "... the mediator of a new covenant... for the redemption of the transgressions that were committed under the first covenant..." (Heb. 9:15; 12:24).

Another important point the author to the Hebrews makes is that the new covenant completely and eternally replaces the old covenant. Since the old covenant was inferior it is "becoming obsolete" (Heb. 8:13), whereas the new covenant is an "eternal covenant" (Heb. 13:20).

The apostle Paul describes the implementation of the new covenant. The way the law of Yahweh is placed on the human heart is by the Spirit of God (II Cor. 3:3). He calls believers "servants of a new covenant" (II Cor. 3:6), and contrasts the fading glory of the old covenant, which abode only in Moses, with the glorious presence of the Spirit of God in believers in the new covenant (II Cor. 3:7-18).

It is very clear the New Testament writers saw Jeremiah's prophecy fulfilled in Jesus Christ. But it is also evident that Jeremiah could not know of such, except to describe a godly leader who would embody all the qualities of David, probably modeled after the Messianic expectations of other prophets (23:5,6; 32:14-16). Again, the New Testament writers were careful to point out that Christ's genealogy was traceable

48

to David, as well as other prominent Old Testament figures (Matt. 1:1-17; Luke 3:23-38).

Regardless of one's interpretation of the fulfillment of the new covenant, he cannot overlook the beauty and wonder of Jeremiah's description of restoration. The pronouncements of judgment were about to culminate in the final overthrow of Jerusalem by the Babylonians. There was no need of further reminders of sin and judgment. Now was the time to provide a broken, humiliated nation a reason to live. Not only would Yahweh sustain them in captivity (29:4-14), but He would gloriously bring them back to Palestine. There would be a new Exodus of the people of Yahweh to once again inhabit the promised land (32:36-44). But this Exodus would have an added blessing; there would be a new and wonderful relationship with the Almighty Lord of the universe:

> "And they shall be My people, and I will be their God; and I will give them one heart and one way, that they may fear Me always, for their own good, and for the good of their children after them.
>
> And I will make an everlasting covenant with them that I will not turn away from them, to do them good; and I will put the fear of Me in their hearts so that they will not turn away from Me."
> 32:38-40

Notes

[1] J.A. Thompson, The New International Commentary on the Old Testament: The Book of Jeremiah, (Grand Rapids: Wm. B. Erdmans Publishing Co., 1980) pg. 555.

[2] C.F. Keil, Commentary on the Old Testament: The Prophecies of Jeremiah, Volume II, (Grand Rapids: Wm. B. Erdmans Publishing Co., 1978), pg. 2.

[3] John Bright, A History of Israel, (Philadelphia: The Westminister Press, 1974), pg. 338.

[4] Bright, pp. 368, 369.

[5] Thompson, pg. 581.

Appendix

Important Dates

931 B.C. - Death of Solomon - Division of the
Kingdom of Israel - Northern and
Southern Kingdoms (Israel and Judah)

722/21 B.C. - The Fall of the Northern Kingdom -
Taken into captivity by Assyria

701 B.C. - Assyrian crisis in Judah - The nation
is miraculously preserved by Yahweh

627 B.C. - The call of Jeremiah during the religious and political reforms of
King Josiah

612 B.C. - The Fall of Assyria - The beginning
of Babylon's rise to power

609 B.C. - Egypt moves against Babylon - Josiah
moves to stop Egypt - Josiah is killed
in battle - Jehoahaz is taken into
captivity by Egypt - Jehoiakim is made king

605 B.C. - Babylon defeats Egypt at Battle of
Charchemish - Babylon takes over
Egyptian conquests (Judah) and takes
some of Judah's leaders to serve in
Babylon among whom was Daniel

598/87 B.C. - Jehoiakim rebells against Babylon -
Jerusalem is besieged - Jehoiakim
dies - Jehoiachin becomes king and
surrenders - He and many others are
taken into captivity - Zedekiah is
made king

586 B.C. - Zedekiah rebells - Babylon destroys
Jerusalem and the Temple and takes
most of Judah into captivity

535 B.C. - King Cyrus of Persia allows the Jews in captivity in Babylon to return to Palestine

Enacted Parables

5:1-6   **Looking for an Honest Man**
           <u>Command</u> - Roam Jerusalem looking
            for an honest man
           <u>Enactment</u> - Jeremiah went and found
            only dishonest, corrupt men
           <u>Interpretation</u> - Because of this
            corruption Judah will be destroyed

13:1-11   **The Linen Waistband**
           <u>Command</u> - Take a linen waistband
            (for priests) to the Euphrates
            and bury it
           <u>Enactment</u> - He buried it and later
            went back to get it
           <u>Interpretation</u> - As the waistband
            was destroyed so Yahweh will
            destroy Judah because they "left"
            Yahweh to serve other gods

16:1-4   **Celibacy**
           <u>Command</u> - Jeremiah was not to marry
            anyone of Judah
           <u>Enactment</u> - He remained single
           <u>Interpretation</u> - The people of Judah
            will die for their sins

16:5-13   **No Mourning or Feasting**
           <u>Command</u> - Jeremiah was not to mourn
            for the dead or feast with them
           <u>Enactment</u> - He refused their fellow-
            ship
           <u>Interpretation</u> - This breaking of
            fellowship symbolized Yahweh's
            rejection of them

18:1-12   **The Potter and the Clay**
           <u>Command</u> - Jeremiah is sent to a
            potter's house
           <u>Enactment</u> - He goes and sees the
            potter re-make a marred vessel

Interpretation - Yahweh will break
in judgment the people and Jerusalem and remold them as He desires

25:15-29   The Cup of Yahweh's Wrath
Command - Jeremiah is to preach
(give the cup) the wrath of
Yahweh on the foreign nations
Enactment - Jeremiah proclaims
judgment against these nations
Interpretation - As a person is
filled with wine so the foreign
nations will be "filled" with
Yahweh's wrath

Chapters 27,28   The Wooden Yoke
Command - Jeremiah was to fashion
a wooden yoke for himself and
preach to the surrounding
nations
Enactment - Jeremiah wears the yoke
and preaches to the emissaries
from the surrounding nations
gathered in Jerusalem
Interpretation - All nations must
serve Babylon

32:1-15   The Purchase of Land
Command - Jeremiah was to buy prop-
erty in Judah from his cousin
Enactment - Jeremiah buys the land
for seventeen shekels
Interpretation - Yahweh will restore
the land after the captivity

35:1-19   The Temptation of the Rechabites
Command - Jeremiah was to give the
leaders of the Rechabite tribe
wine to drink
Enactment - He takes them to a chamber
of the Temple, near the officials,
and gives them wine. They refuse
to drink it.
Interpretation - These Rechabites
have better followed their ancestors'

vow to not drink wine than
Judah has its vow to obey
Yahweh; therefore, judgment
will come

43:8-13   The Hiding of the Stones
        Command - Jeremiah was to hide
          some stones at Pharoah's palace
        Enactment - He hides the stones at
          the entrance of the palace with
          some Jews watching
        Interpretation - Nebuchadnezzar will
          conquer Egypt

51:59-64   The Scroll into the Euphrates
        Command - Jeremiah commands Seraiah
          the quartermaster to take a scroll
          with Yahweh's judgment of Babylon
          written on it into captivity with
          him
        Enactment - Seraiah was to take the
          scroll, read it to the captives
          in Babylon, tie a rock to it, and
          throw it into the Euphrates
        Interpretation - Babylon will sink
          like the scroll because of Yahweh's
          judgment

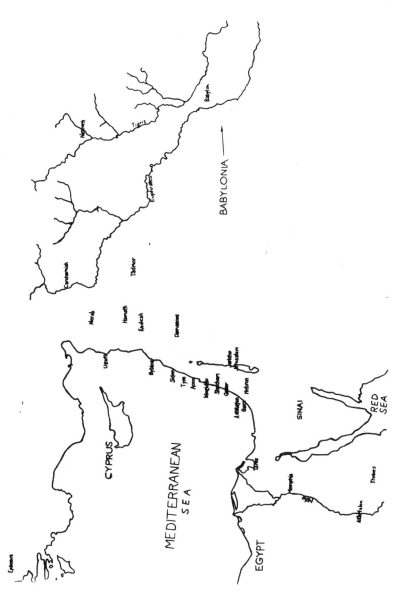

MEDITERRANEAN
S E A

BABYLONIA →

CYPRUS

EGYPT

SINAI

RED
SEA

Babylon

Tigris

Nineveh

Euphrates

Carchemish

Tadmor

Arvad

Hamath

Kadesh

Damascus

Ugarit

Byblos

Sidon

Tyre

Acco

Megiddo

Shechem

Gezer

Salem/Jerusalem

Jericho

Hebron

Ashkelon

Gaza

Tanis

Memphis

Akhetaton

Thebes

Sardis

Ephesus

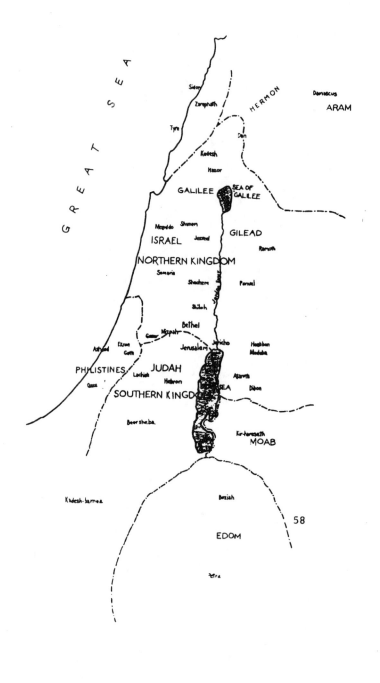

Selected Bibliography

Bright, John. A History of Israel. Philadelphia:
    The Westminister Press, 1974.

Blackwood, A.W., Jr. Commentary on Jeremiah.
    Waco, TX.: Word Books, 1977.

Calvin, John. Calvin's Commentaries. volumes 9, 10.

Cunliffe, Jones, H. Jeremiah (Torch), 1960.

Harrison, R.K. Jeremiah and Lamentations. Down-
    ers Grove, Ill.: Inter-Varsity Press, 1973.

Huey, F.B. Yesterday's Prophets for Today's
    World. Nashville: Broadman Press, 1980.

Jensen, Irving. Jeremiah and Lamentations.
    Chicago: Mood Press, 1974.

Keil, C.F. The Prophecies of Jeremiah: Keil and
    Delitzsch Old Testament Commentaries, vol.8.
    Grand Rapids: Wm. B. Erdmans Publishing
    Co., 1978.

Leslie, E.A. Jeremiah. New York: Abingdon
    Press, 1954.

Pfeiffer, Charles F. Old Testament History.
    Grand Rapids: Baker Book House, 1979.

Streane, A.W. Jeremiah and Lamentations: Cam-
    bridge Bible for Schools and Colleges.
    Cambridge University Press, 1887.

Thompson, J.A. The Book of Jeremiah. Grand
    Rapids: Wm. B. Erdmans Publishing Co.,
    1980.

Wiseman, D.J. Illustrations from Biblical
    Archaeology. Grand Rapids: Wm. B. Erdmans
    Publishing Co., 1958.

Young, E.J.   An Introduction to the Old Testa-
      ment.   Grand Rapids: Wm. B. Erdmans Pub-
      lishing Co., 1977.

_____.   My Servants the Prophets.   Grand
      Rapids: Wm. B. Erdmans Publishing Co.,
      1978.

Index

Steven M. Fettke is a native of Alva, Oklahoma and received his B.A. from Northwestern Oklahoma State University. He obtained an M.Div. from Southwestern Baptist Theological Seminary in Ft. Worth, Texas, and is currently working on his Ph.D. in Old Testament Studies. He and his wife Lorraine (Tilly) live in Lakeland, Florida where he teaches Bible courses at Southeastern College.